Original title:
Pieces of Me

Copyright © 2024 Swan Charm
All rights reserved.

Author: Sebastian Sarapuu
ISBN HARDBACK: 978-9916-79-161-5
ISBN PAPERBACK: 978-9916-79-162-2
ISBN EBOOK: 978-9916-79-163-9

Grace Amidst the Gaps

In shadows cast by doubt and fear,
The light of hope draws ever near.
Through trials deep and valleys wide,
Your grace, O Lord, shall be our guide.

When burdens weigh upon our hearts,
And weariness from faith departs,
We seek Your peace, our souls to mend,
In every break, Your love descend.

From broken paths, new blooms arise,
Each tear a prayer that lifts us high.
In every gap, Your mercy pours,
A promise kept, forever yours.

The whispers of Your gentle call,
Remind us, Lord, we're not that small.
For in the cracks where shadows lie,
Your grace illuminates the sky.

So here we stand, in faith so bold,
With stories rich, and hearts of gold.
In grace we walk, in peace we dwell,
Amidst the gaps, our souls compel.

The Covenant of the Cracked

In the fissures of earth, the promise lies,
Whispers of faith beneath fractured skies.
Each scar a testament, a story unfolds,
In every broken path, sacred truth beholds.

Beneath the shattered stones, hope does bloom,
Light finds its way through the temples of gloom.
With each step forward, we rise from despair,
In the covenant forged, love's essence we share.

Binds of Belief

Chains of our hearts, in prayer they unite,
Hymns of devotion, lifting us to the light.
In stillness we gather, in echoes we stand,
Binding our souls by the grace of His hand.

Through trials and tempest, our spirits grow strong,
In the forge of the faithful, we sing our song.
Each bond that we form, a divine melody,
In the tapestry woven, His love sets us free.

Shadows of Surrender

In valleys of doubt, we cast down our pride,
Letting the shadows in meekness abide.
With open hearts bare, we offer our fears,
In the silence of trust, our burden disappears.

To kneel in the dawn brings a peace like a stream,
As darkness gives way to a luminous dream.
In surrender we find what the heart truly seeks,
A whisper of grace in the stillness that speaks.

Celestial Fragments

Stars woven bright in the fabric of night,
Glimmers of hope, like prayers taking flight.
Each fragment a journey from distant afar,
Lingering truths, like the glow of a star.

As we trace the heavens, our spirits ignite,
In unity found, we reflect His pure light.
Through celestial whispers, our lives intertwine,
In the dance of the cosmos, divine plans align.

Celestial Footprints

In the stillness of night,
Stars whisper their grace,
Guiding lost souls home,
To a sacred embrace.

Pathways of light unfurl,
Beneath the endless sky,
Each step a story told,
Of moments passing by.

Echoes of ancient hymns,
Resound in gentle winds,
Hearts dance in unity,
As love always mends.

Through valleys dark and deep,
We traverse with no fear,
Hand in hand with the Divine,
Our purpose crystal clear.

In every breath we take,
Celestial whispers blend,
Leaving footprints of hope,
As we ascend, ascend.

Mosaic of Memories

Fragments of light and shade,
Stitched by heavenly hands,
Each moment a vibrant thread,
In the tapestry of lands.

Threads of joy and sorrow,
Interwoven with grace,
A mosaic of memories,
A heart's sacred place.

In the quiet of morning,
Dreams dance on the breeze,
Whispers of the Creator,
Usher forth inner peace.

Time flows like a river,
Through mountains, through plains,
Each memory a stepping stone,
In love's gentle reigns.

With faith as our canvas,
And hope in our hearts,
We paint with devotion,
As each new day starts.

Soul's Reverence

In silence, the spirit speaks,
A melody divine,
Resounding in the chambers,
Where light and love entwine.

Each heartbeat is a prayer,
Ascending to the skies,
Offering gratitude,
With every breath that sighs.

Through valleys of compassion,
We journey, hand in hand,
With courage as our compass,
Together we shall stand.

In the depths of our being,
The sacred truth ignites,
Illuminating paths,
In the darkest of nights.

Reverence blooms within,
A sacred, silent flame,
Guiding our souls onward,
In the Spirit's name.

Divine Unraveling

In the fabric of existence,
Threads of faith unwind,
Revealing the great mystery,
That binds all humankind.

With each moment unfolding,
We glimpse the sacred plan,
In the dance of the cosmos,
In the touch of the hand.

Embraced by creation's heart,
We search for what is true,
Divine unravelling secrets,
In each shade and hue.

Through trials, we find wisdom,
In the shadows we grow,
As rivers of grace flow,
In the eternal glow.

Together, we discover,
The light in every soul,
In the divine unravelling,
We become beautifully whole.

Fragments of Grace

In quiet moments, hearts take flight,
Each breath a gift, in sacred light.
The path unfolds, unknown yet clear,
Embrace the love that draws us near.

Through trials faced, we learn to see,
The strength bestowed, a mystery.
In every tear, a lesson shines,
A tapestry of love divine.

In whispered prayers, we find our way,
Each fragment leads, come what may.
With open hearts, we share our grace,
Together we seek our sacred place.

Shattered Reflections

In broken mirrors, truth can gleam,
Pieces scattered, like a dream.
From darkness comes a light so bright,
Healing whispers, soft as night.

Each shard reveals a story spun,
Of battles fought and victories won.
In shattered forms, we find our truce,
A sacred dance, our heart's excuse.

From cracks in faith, new colors rise,
A luminous dawn in tear-streaked skies.
We gather strength from past's embrace,
In every break, we find our grace.

Whispers of the Soul

In silence deep, the heart will sing,
A song of hope in everything.
The soul's soft murmurs, sweet refrain,
In gentle breezes, love's sustain.

Through trials harsh, we learn to flow,
In every storm, new seeds we sow.
With every whisper, truth unfolds,
In sacred spaces, it consoles.

So listen close, let your heart be still,
In quietude, find peace and will.
The whispers guide, they lead us home,
In love's embrace, no need to roam.

Mosaic of Faith

In colors bright, our spirits blend,
A sacred mosaic, hand in hand.
Each tile a story, rich and rare,
Together woven, love laid bare.

Through struggles shared, our bond does grow,
In every piece, a truth we know.
The beauty found in our embrace,
In unity, we find our place.

Trust in the journey, step by step,
With every heartbeat, joy inept.
A tapestry of faith unveiled,
In every heart, His love has sailed.

Seraphic Splinters

In sacred light where shadows play,
The seraphs sing both night and day.
With wings of grace, they softly tread,
Embracing all the words unsaid.

Upon the path of faith we strive,
In unity, our hopes revive.
Every heart a flickering flame,
In love's embrace, we seek His name.

With whispered prayers that rise like smoke,
In softened tones, the Spirit spoke.
Each splinter shines with holy fire,
Our souls aflame, our hearts aspire.

Through trials faced and burdens borne,
In humble trust, we are reborn.
To serve the light and walk in grace,
In seraph's song, we find our place.

Pilgrimage of the Soul

On pilgrim path, we travel far,
Guided by hope, our guiding star.
With every step on sacred ground,
In faith, we soar, our hearts unbound.

Through valleys low and mountains high,
With whispered prayers that touch the sky.
In quiet moments, we align,
Our souls entwined, the Divine sign.

Each mile we walk, a lesson learned,
In trials faced, our hearts have yearned.
The journey carved through time and space,
In every heart, we seek His grace.

With every dawn, the light appears,
A echo of forgotten years.
In pilgrimage, our spirits glow,
As love's soft whisper guides us home.

Amongst the Ashes of Reverence

In shadows cast by flickering light,
We gather close 'neath stars so bright.
Amongst the ashes, prayers arise,
Transforming pain to sacred ties.

With every tear, a story flows,
In reverence deep, our spirit knows.
From burnt-out dreams, new hopes emerge,
A cycle of life where hearts converge.

In silent awe, we bow our heads,
Accepting both the roads we tread.
From dust and grace, our truths shall sing,
Finding strength in each offering.

Amongst the ashes, love will reign,
Through storms of doubt and waves of pain.
In sacred trust, we rise anew,
Embracing life, both born and true.

Beseeching the Broken

Beseeching hearts, we lift our cries,
In brokenness, our spirit flies.
With every burden that we bear,
In unity, we find our prayer.

Through shattered dreams and silent fears,
We weave a tapestry of tears.
Each hurt, a thread, each pain, a part,
In love's embrace, we mend the heart.

The light still shines through cracks and scars,
A testament beneath the stars.
With faith as balm, we seek the whole,
In every wound, the healer's goal.

In whispers soft, our hopes ascend,
Beseeching grace that knows no end.
For in the fractures, beauty grows,
In brokenness, His love bestows.

Silent Songs of the Heart

In whispers soft, the spirit speaks,
A melody of grace it seeks.
In shadows deep, the light does dance,
Awakening the soul's romance.

Through prayer's embrace, the stillness grows,
A tranquil stream where silence flows.
Each longing note, a sacred song,
In love's sweet truth, where we belong.

Beneath the stars, the silence gleams,
In twilight's hush, we trace our dreams.
An echo stirs within the night,
Reflecting all that brings us light.

From hearts aflame, our whispers rise,
To realms unseen, beyond the skies.
In gratitude, we hum in peace,
A covenant that will not cease.

Embers of the Sacred

In the quiet glow, the embers spark,
A flame for faith, igniting dark.
With every breath, we fan the fire,
In sacred space, our hearts aspire.

The warmth of hope, it weaves a thread,
Connecting souls where angels tread.
In reverence, we bow our heads,
To honor paths our spirit treads.

Each flicker tells of journeys past,
Of light that shone when shadows cast.
We gather close, a circle bound,
In unity, where love is found.

Through trials faced, the flames will rise,
Transforming pain into the prize.
With every spark, a promise made,
To light the way when night has laid.

Woven in Reverence

In threads of gold, our lives entwine,
A tapestry of souls divine.
With every stitch, a prayer bestowed,
In sacred patterns, our love glowed.

From humble roots, we draw our strength,
In unity, we find our breadth.
With reverent hands, we weave and spin,
A legacy of where we've been.

Each color speaks of trials faced,
A journey rich with love embraced.
In woven hearts, we rise anew,
In every hue, a promise true.

Through life's design, we seek the light,
In shadows cast, we join the fight.
With reverence held, we stand as one,
A sacred bond that can't be undone.

The Divine Within

In every heartbeat, life unfolds,
The sacred truth that love beholds.
Awakening the light inside,
In stillness, we find the divine guide.

With open hearts, we seek and find,
The quiet voice that stirs the mind.
Within the chaos, peace will bloom,
In depths of silence, we shed gloom.

With every breath, the soul takes flight,
In whispers soft, it claims the light.
In sacred space, our spirits soar,
Embracing all that came before.

The spark of God in each of us,
A sacred bond, profound and thus.
In loving grace, we find our worth,
The divine within, our heart's rebirth.

Tapestry of Reverence

In the stillness of dawn,
The whispers of faith arise,
Threads of love intertwine,
In the heart's sacred ties.

Mountains bow in silence,
As prayers float through the air,
Each heartbeat a promise,
A testament to care.

Stars light the night sky,
Guiding souls lost in the dark,
In every flicker we see,
The Divine's gentle spark.

Rivers flow with purpose,
Carrying dreams like a song,
In their depths we discover,
Where the faithful belong.

With every breath taken,
A symphony of grace,
In this tapestry woven,
Together we find our place.

Fragments of the Divine

In the garden of existence,
Petals fall like soft prayers,
Each fragment a moment,
In the stillness that cares.

The sun kisses the horizon,
Gold spilling on the ground,
In its light, we find healing,
In silence, wisdom profound.

Clouds drift like thoughts,
Over valleys calm and wide,
In their shadows we wander,
With our faith as our guide.

Fireflies dance in twilight,
A chorus of glowing grace,
In this fragile display,
Divine beauty we embrace.

Each fragment a blessing,
Scattered across our way,
In the heart of creation,
Love's light will always stay.

Echoes of the Heart

Beneath a vast sky,
Hearts beat with gentle trust,
In the echoes of love,
We find strength in the dust.

Through valleys of sorrow,
The spirit whispers low,
In the shadows of pain,
Seeds of hope, we sow.

Raindrops sing soft hymns,
On the leaves, they alight,
In their rhythm we hear,
God's promise in the night.

Mountains rise in glory,
Standing firm through the years,
In their grace, we discover,
A balm for our fears.

Every echo reminds us,
In the stillness, we seek,
The pulse of a journey,
That makes us both strong and weak.

Illuminated Shadows

In the twilight's embrace,
Shadows dance on the ground,
Each step a reflection,
Of the light that is found.

Stars flicker like lanterns,
Guiding souls on their way,
In the dark, we discover,
Hope's gentle sway.

Whispers in the silence,
Carry prayers to the night,
In every breath we take,
We find faith in the fight.

The moon, a silver cradle,
Cradling dreams of the bold,
In her glow, we gather,
Stories waiting to be told.

Illuminated shadows,
Teach us to be aware,
In the dance of the light,
Grace flows everywhere.

The Alchemy of Grace

In silent whispers, grace unfolds,
Transforming hearts, turning souls.
From ashes rise, a vibrant hue,
In love's embrace, we are made new.

The gold of faith in trials found,
In humble prayers, our hopes abound.
We seek the light through darkest night,
In every tear, a spark ignites.

The potter's hands, they shape our fate,
In every struggle, love won't wait.
Through hands that heal and hearts that mend,
The cycle of grace will never end.

With every breath, we sing His praise,
In every moment, dance in grace.
From brokenness, we find our part,
In alchemy, we blend our heart.

In unity, we'll walk this path,
Embracing joy, and also wrath.
For in the trials, we become whole,
In grace's arms, we find our role.

In the Shadow of His Love

Beneath the wings of love divine,
In shadows soft, our spirits shine.
With every breath, He draws us near,
In whispers sweet, dispelling fear.

From depths of grace, our burdens fall,
In love's embrace, we hear the call.
Transformed by peace that knows no end,
In every heart, His light extends.

In trials faced, we find His hand,
In every storm, we choose to stand.
Through valleys low and mountains high,
In every tear, our spirits fly.

His mercy rains, like gentle streams,
In quiet moments, hope redeems.
In shadows deep, His love does flow,
A guiding light, we come to know.

Together bound, our hearts aligned,
In every heartbeat, love defined.
In unity, we rise above,
Forever anchored in His love.

Sanctified Fragments

In shattered dreams, we find the grace,
Each broken piece, a sacred place.
From every scar, a story told,
In unity, our hearts behold.

Through fractured lives, the light will shine,
In every crack, His love divine.
With open hands, we lift our soul,
In every fragment, we are whole.

Through trials faced, our spirits soar,
In every struggle, we implore.
The hands of time will mold our heart,
In every end, a brand new start.

With faith we weave a tapestry,
In every thread, His mystery.
In moments lost, His truth we find,
Our sanctified hearts, intertwined.

Together bound, in love we shine,
In Christ alone, our light aligns.
In every piece, redemption sings,
In sanctified fragments, hope takes wing.

Tidal Waves of Grace

Like waves that crash upon the shore,
His grace abounds forevermore.
In currents strong, we find our place,
In oceans deep, we know His grace.

Each surge that flows, a gift bestowed,
In storms we trust, He is our road.
With every tide, we rise anew,
In love's embrace, His promise true.

From depths unknown, our spirits rise,
In every breath, a sweet surprise.
Through raging seas, we walk by faith,
In tidal waves, we find our waith.

In rhythmic dance, the waters sway,
In grace's flow, we find our way.
With open hearts, we seek His face,
In tidal waves, we know His grace.

Together bound, like ships at sea,
In every wave, we find the key.
In unity, our hearts embrace,
Tidal waves of love, eternal grace.

Celestial Mosaic

In the tapestry of stars, we find,
Threads of grace, gently entwined.
Heaven's light upon us falls,
Guiding souls through sacred halls.

Whispers of the night unfold,
Stories of the meek and bold.
Each heartbeat a prayer, a song,
In the unity, we belong.

Nature sings a holy hymn,
In the shadows, we search within.
Every leaf, a sacred word,
In each moment, the divine stirred.

Mountains rise, a testament,
To the love that heaven sent.
In valleys deep, the spirit dwells,
Echoing ancient, timeless bells.

With every dawn, we rise anew,
In the mosaic, the heart is true.
Celestial whispers guide our way,
In unity, we humbly pray.

Sacred Echoes

In the silence, hear the call,
Echoes of the One in all.
Through the stillness, spirits soar,
In each soul, a sacred core.

Moments pause, the heart awaits,
Love eternal, that radiates.
Every prayer a flickering flame,
Uniting us in sacred name.

With every step on hallowed ground,
Presence felt, the lost are found.
In the shadows, faith ignites,
Guiding us through darkest nights.

Voices rise in harmony,
An ancient hymn, our unity.
Through the ages, truth has led,
In the echoes, the heart is fed.

In every tear, the joy bestowed,
In our hearts, the love bestowed.
Through sacred echoes, spirits free,
In this chorus, we shall be.

Voice of the Spirit

In the stillness, hear the sound,
The spirit's whisper all around.
Voices soft, like morning dew,
  Gently calling, calling you.

Rising tides of faith and grace,
Leading hearts to sacred space.
In the silence, truth reveals,
The love of God, it softly heals.

Stars above, a guiding light,
Illuminating darkest night.
With each breath, we feel the lead,
The voice of spirit, daily fed.

Language pure, no need for tongues,
In every heart, the song it thrums.
Harmony in sacred trust,
We are dust, and yet we must.

Journey onward, spirits soar,
On this path, forevermore.
In unity, we lift our choice,
Together hear the spirit's voice.

Shattered Sanctuaries

In the ruins where hope seems lost,
Shattered dreams pay a heavy cost.
Yet in ashes, life can bloom,
From darkness, we will find our room.

Within the fractures, light can seep,
In brokenness, our spirits leap.
Every battle, a chance to grow,
From shattered sanctuaries, love will flow.

Tears that fall, like sacred rain,
Washing over every pain.
In each sorrow, grace begins,
Through the trials, the spirit wins.

Through the storms, the heart remains,
In the chaos, love sustains.
Rebuilding walls with whispered prayer,
Sanctuaries rise from despair.

From rubble, faith ignites and shines,
In every heart, the love entwines.
In shattered places, hope will rise,
Like a phoenix, touch the skies.

Threads of Grace

In quiet dawn, the light descends,
A tapestry of love extends.
Each thread intertwined with care,
Weaving hope through whispered prayer.

With gentle hands, the Spirit guides,
Through valleys deep where sorrow hides.
In every heart, a spark ignites,
Threads of grace embrace our fights.

The broken souls, like shards of glass,
Reflecting truths that come to pass.
In every tear, a chance to mend,
The sacred journey has no end.

Lifted voices, we raise our song,
In unity, we all belong.
Together seeking, finding peace,
Threads of grace that never cease.

So, trust the path that's yet to unfold,
In the heart's whispers, truths are told.
With faith, we'll stand through night and day,
Bound by love, we'll find our way.

Celestial Whispers

Beneath the stars, the heavens breathe,
Soft murmurs weave, as angels seethe.
With every twinkle, a promise speaks,
Guiding hearts in the light it leaks.

In silent nights, the spirit calls,
Through shadowed lands, where darkness falls.
Each whispered prayer, a soft embrace,
Echoing light from a sacred place.

The moonlight dances on gentle streams,
A song of hope, a thread of dreams.
In cosmic realms, love's light expands,
Embracing souls within its hands.

In sacred spaces, hearts align,
With celestial whispers, love divine.
A truth revealed in every sigh,
Connecting earth to the endless sky.

So lift your gaze to skies so vast,
In fleeting moments, find peace at last.
For in the stillness, grace appears,
Celestial whispers calm our fears.

Heart's Labyrinth

In the maze of thoughts where shadows dwell,
Each corner turned, a hidden spell.
Through winding paths, the heart will roam,
Seeking solace, finding home.

In tangled threads of joy and pain,
A journey deep, like fallen rain.
With every step, the lessons grow,
In heart's labyrinth, love's light glows.

The whispers echo through the night,
Guiding lost souls toward the light.
Each choice we make, a sacred art,
A dance of faith that shapes the heart.

In moments still, the truth reveals,
The depth of love that always heals.
Through every trial, we find our way,
In heart's labyrinth, we learn to stay.

So trust the path that God designed,
For in each twist, His love you'll find.
With open hearts, we'll walk with grace,
In heart's labyrinth, we find our place.

Tattered Prayers

Upon the altar, tattered prayers,
Whispers of hope, cast on the stairs.
In every word, a story told,
In frayed edges, a heart of gold.

With trembling hands, they rise like smoke,
In silent nights, their truths evoke.
For every tear, a seed is sown,
In brokenness, true strength is grown.

The echoes linger in the air,
A testament of love and care.
In every sigh, our spirits soar,
Tattered prayers, forevermore.

Through darkest times, we seek the light,
In faith, we find the courage to fight.
With every struggle, a prayer ascends,
Embracing all that the heart defends.

So gather close, with hearts laid bare,
In unity, we lift our prayer.
For in the fabric of our days,
We find the beauty in tattered ways.

Chords of Faith

In the stillness, spirits rise,
Embraced by light, the heart replies.
With every breath, a song we weave,
In faith we stand, trusting, believe.

Through trials faced, our souls ignite,
Guided by grace, we find our light.
Hands entwined, we walk the path,
In love's embrace, dispelling wrath.

Whispers linger in the air,
A sacred bond, a heartfelt prayer.
In unity, we find our strength,
For faith transcends all worldly length.

With every note, our spirits soar,
In harmony, we seek for more.
The chords of life, a melody,
In love and light, we find the key.

Together, we shall rise anew,
With hearts ablaze, we follow through.
Faith as our compass, we'll not stray,
In divine purpose, come what may.

Alchemy of Being

In quietude, the spirit gleams,
Transforming shadows into dreams.
From earth to sky, we rise and flow,
In alchemy, our essence grow.

The breath of life, a sacred gift,
In every moment, spirits lift.
Through trials faced, we learn to see,
The alchemy of being free.

As golden rays embrace the dawn,
In nature's arms, we are reborn.
With every heartbeat, love's decree,
In unity, we find the key.

The sacred dance of time and grace,
Within our hearts, we find our place.
For through the fire, our truth we claim,
In alchemy, we are one flame.

With open hearts, we dare to dream,
In silence, hear the universe's theme.
The alchemy of life unveils,
In every breath, love never fails.

Sacred Whispers

In the hush of twilight's grace,
Sacred whispers, a warm embrace.
The gentle touch of the divine,
In every heart, a love that shines.

Through the valleys, darkness veils,
Yet hope arises, the spirit sails.
In quiet moments, truth does speak,
With sacred whispers, we are meek.

The winds of change, they softly tell,
In every story, a holy spell.
In the tapestry of time, we weave,
With sacred whispers, we believe.

Glimmers of light break through the night,
In fearlessness, we seek the light.
Listening closely, hearts align,
In sacred whispers, love divine.

With every prayer, a soft reply,
In silence, we expand and fly.
Sacred whispers guide our way,
In peace and love, we find our stay.

Intimate Offerings

In dawn's embrace, we give our all,
With open hearts, we heed the call.
Each tear we shed, a sacred gift,
In intimate offerings, spirits lift.

The altar of our humble heart,
In every moment, we play our part.
With whispers soft, our souls connect,
In intimate trust, we reflect.

Through trials faced, our faith expands,
In unity, we join our hands.
With every breath, we share our dreams,
In intimate offerings, love redeems.

Each moment spent in mindful grace,
In the silence, we find our place.
For love abounds in every thought,
In intimate offerings, we are caught.

With gratitude, we face the day,
In every act, love leads the way.
Intimate offerings, pure and right,
In sacred bonds, we find our light.

Masks of Salvation

In shadows deep, the masks we wear,
Hide truth from those who seek and care.
Yet beneath these painted smiles,
A heart cries out for love's soft miles.

With every face, a new disguise,
Divine reflections, sacred ties.
To pull away the veils of night,
Is to reveal the inner light.

In faith we find the strength to tear,
The shrouded fears we choose to bear.
For grace unfolds when we embrace,
The open arms of love's true grace.

So let us wear our truth with pride,
In vulnerability, we confide.
The masks, they fade in love's bright glow,
Salvation's path, we come to know.

Together in this sacred space,
We lift each other, face to face.
With open hearts, we take the chance,
To find our peace in faith's sweet dance.

Vows of the Heart

In silent whispers, vows are sworn,
A promise made, a bond reborn.
Through trials faced and joys we weave,
In sacred trust, we achieve.

Each heartbeat sings a solemn tune,
A hymn of love beneath the moon.
In every tear, a lesson learned,
In every joy, a fire burned.

With hands entwined, we pray as one,
To walk in grace until we're done.
The vows we speak in quiet prayer,
Resound in faith, a truth we share.

Through storms and light, our spirits rise,
In love's embrace, we see the skies.
For every promise, small or grand,
Is rooted deep, a holy strand.

In moments sweet, in times of strife,
We find the heart of sacred life.
These vows, they echo, strong and clear,
Together bound, we persevere.

Lanterns in the Dark

When shadows fall and darkness creeps,
Our lanterns glow, the promise keeps.
Through trials faced, the path is shown,
In faith we find we're not alone.

A flicker bright, a guiding star,
Illuminates those lost afar.
With every step, our spirits soar,
Through love's warm light, we seek for more.

In darkest hours, we light the way,
With prayerful hearts, we choose to stay.
As lanterns burn, they hold our fears,
And turn them into joyful tears.

Together we shall walk this night,
With every soul, a spark of light.
In unity, our hearts will part,
Embracing all, we play our part.

As dawn will break and darkness fades,
We gather strength from love's cascades.
Our lanterns shine through every storm,
In sacred light, our hearts grow warm.

Sacred Rebirth

In silence deep, the soul takes flight,
A sacred journey into the light.
From ashes rise, a spirit new,
In every breath, we start anew.

The past we cherish, the lessons learned,
In love's embrace, our hearts are burned.
With every tear, a new seed sown,
In sacred ground, a love has grown.

Through trials faced, our spirits mend,
In unity, we find our end.
With faith as guide, we break the shell,
To share our truth, our life to tell.

The dawn will break, our colors bloom,
In harmony, we shun the gloom.
A sacred rebirth, pure and grand,
Anchored deep in love's warm hand.

So let us rise, and sing our song,
In every heart, where we belong.
Transcend the darkness, embrace the light,
In sacred rebirth, we find our flight.

Soulful Reverberations

In silence deep, the spirit calls,
Through night so dark, the whisper falls.
Echoes of love in heart's embrace,
A dance of light, in sacred space.

With every breath, the promise grows,
A tapestry where faith bestows.
In trials faced, the soul takes flight,
Toward the dawn, a quest for light.

The river flows, of hope anew,
Cleansed by grace, our souls imbue.
In harmony, we find our way,
As sacred truths unite to stay.

With fervent prayer, we rise as one,
Reciting verses that can't be undone.
In unity, we lift our voice,
Reverberate, we all rejoice.

So linger close, and hear the sound,
Of love divine that knows no bound.
With hearts aglow, we spread the light,
A soulful path, forever bright.

Threads of the Ethereal

Woven in time, the threads align,
A sacred tapestry, pure and divine.
In twilight's glow, we dance and weave,
A timeless love, we come to believe.

From shadows cast, the light breaks through,
Each strand a story, each hue a view.
In quiet moments, reflections gleam,
Ethereal threads, stitched with a dream.

The fabric soft, like whispers of grace,
Embracing souls in its warm embrace.
Through trials and joy, the fibers strain,
Yet beauty emerges in joy and pain.

In divinity, we find our place,
A dance of spirits, a cosmic chase.
With every thread, a journey sought,
In ethereal realms, love is brought.

So let us mend what fate may fray,
With threads entwined, we find our way.
With hearts uplifted, hand in hand,
In unity, forever we'll stand.

Unveiling Sacred Desolation

Amidst the ruins, the heart still sighs,
In sacred spaces, where spirit lies.
From ashes cold, new life will bloom,
In desolation, a chance to groom.

Bearing the weight of trials unknown,
Each crack and crevice, the truth has shown.
In darkest hours, the light shall pierce,
Unveiling hope, whispers to hear.

The barren land, though seemingly lost,
Holds secrets deep, yet to be tossed.
In solitude, we find our voice,
A call to rise, to make a choice.

Through shattered dreams, the spirit thrives,
In sacred desolation, the soul arrives.
With every breath, we brave the night,
Awakening to eternal light.

So let us wander through the bleak,
In search of wisdom, the heart will speak.
Though trials test, and hope feels thin,
In desolation's arms, we learn to begin.

Ethereal Residue

In realms unseen, the echoes cling,
Like hidden dust, on angel's wing.
Whispers of past in shadows lay,
Ethereal residue, come what may.

From stardust formed, our spirits flow,
In fragile dreams, where stories grow.
In softest sighs, our hopes remain,
Ethereal traces, love's sweet gain.

Through trials faced, the lessons taught,
In every tear, our courage bought.
From heart to heart, the light will gleam,
In sacred moments, we find our dream.

So gently tread on paths divine,
In residue of love, we intertwine.
With open hearts, we seek the glow,
Ethereal bonds, forever flow.

In twilight's hush, we feel the grace,
Of ancient truths in time and space.
So cherish well the whispers small,
Ethereal residue, embraces all.

Heartstrings of Faith

In shadows deep, the whispers call,
Trust in the light, let not heart fall.
With every prayer, a hope is sowed,
Through trials faced, our spirits flowed.

A sacred bond, entwined so tight,
In faith we gather, igniting the light.
Hearts united, a chorus strong,
In love's embrace, we all belong.

Through valleys low, on mountains high,
With every tear, we learn to fly.
The journey long, yet never lost,
For every gain, a noble cost.

In silent nights, our souls entwine,
In melodies soft, divine, they shine.
The heartstrings play, a tune so sweet,
In faith we walk, in love we meet.

In every sigh, the heavens hear,
With every doubt, we hold so dear.
For faith, a treasure, in hearts we keep,
A promise made, forever deep.

A Symphony of Silence

In quietude where spirits soar,
The gentle hush reveals much more.
In silence wrapped, we find our way,
Through whispered prayers, night turns to day.

Upon the breeze, a sacred song,
In stillness held, where we belong.
With every breath, a calm unfolds,
In silence pure, the truth retold.

The heart beats soft, a sacred drum,
In moments still, our souls succumb.
A symphony, without a sound,
In silence deep, our hearts are found.

In twilight's glow, the heavens speak,
In gentle tones, for those who seek.
In quiet corners, where shadows dance,
In silence profound, we find our chance.

The world outside may rage and roar,
Yet in the stillness, we explore.
A sanctuary, our spirits lift,
In silent grace, a holy gift.

The Sanctuary Within

A temple built of hopes and dreams,
In silent chambers, love redeems.
Within these walls, our whispers rise,
In hidden depths, the spirit flies.

Through trials faced, the heart can mend,
In sacred space, we find our friends.
Together held, we rise anew,
In faith's embrace, we journey through.

The sanctuary, a place of peace,
Where every burden finds release.
In every laugh, in every tear,
The light of love draws ever near.

A guardian of the soul's delight,
In every shadow, shines the light.
With every step, a path we trace,
In quietude, we find our grace.

In gentle whispers, hearts align,
Within the walls, divinely fine.
A refuge made, a home to dwell,
In this sanctuary, all is well.

Glimmers of the Infinite

In starlit skies, the heavens gleam,
Each spark a promise, every dream.
Through cosmic eyes, we see the light,
In every shadow, shines the bright.

With open hearts, we seek the truth,
In every moment, a childlike youth.
The universe sings, in harmony,
A cosmic dance, of you and me.

In glimmers soft, the soul awakens,
In every heartbeat, love unshaken.
Through endless realms, our spirits roam,
In every star, we find our home.

The infinite speaks in silent tones,
In every breath, the heart atones.
With every glance towards the skies,
In glimmers bright, the spirit flies.

In unity, we rise and blend,
In every beginning, there is an end.
Yet in this dance, forever flows,
In glimmers of the infinite, love glows.

Fragments of Faith

In every whisper, a prayer flows,
Hearts entwined where the spirit glows.
Though shadows linger, we find our light,
In trust and hope, we stand upright.

Mountains tremble at love's decree,
Guided by hands we cannot see.
Each fragment shines, a sacred part,
Together we weave the tapestry of heart.

Through storms that rage and time that bends,
Our faith endures, a light that mends.
In quiet moments, we hear the call,
A promise made, a love for all.

In pain and joy, in loss and gain,
We gather strength, transcend the pain.
In every struggle, the spirit sings,
A dance of hope that faith always brings.

So lift your eyes to the skies above,
In every breath, embrace the love.
For in these fragments, we find our whole,
The sacred journey of every soul.

The Altar of My Soul

Before the flame of truth I stand,
With trembling heart and open hand.
Each tear a bead, a prayer set free,
On this altar, I come to be.

The whispers of the past ignite,
In every shadow, a glimpse of light.
With humble heart, I lay my fears,
Offering silence mixed with tears.

Around this space, the angels tread,
Each breath a prayer, each word unsaid.
In love's embrace, I find my peace,
A sacred moment, fears release.

The echoes linger, the spirit swells,
In sacred journeys, our story tells.
With every step, my soul ignites,
In faith and hope, the heart unites.

So here I stand, beneath the skies,
The altar holds my soul's true prize.
For in this wonder, we each unroll,
The deep unfolding of the soul.

Echoes of Devotion

In every dawn, the world awakes,
With whispered vows, our spirit shakes.
Through valleys deep and mountains tall,
We rise in faith, we heed the call.

In gentle breezes, grace descends,
With every heartbeat, love extends.
The echoes of our trusting hearts,
Remind us that we're never apart.

When darkness falls and shadows creep,
In prayers of hope, our souls we keep.
With every trial, our hearts refine,
In unity, our spirits align.

Through every struggle, through every strife,
We chase the light, embrace this life.
The echoes of devotion ring,
A melody of grace we bring.

So lift your voice, let love resound,
In every moment, grace is found.
For in devotion, we find our way,
An everlasting song that will stay.

Mosaic of the Divine Within

Each piece a story, a journey told,
In colors bright, in shades of gold.
The mosaic of life, a sacred art,
Holds the heartbeat of every heart.

With every challenge, a fragment shows,
The beauty born where the spirit grows.
In joy and sorrow, we start anew,
A canvas painted in vibrant hue.

The brush of love, it sweeps and glides,
In each connection, the spirit bides.
Through laughter and tears, grace intertwines,
In the dance of life, the divine shines.

So let us gather, these pieces rare,
In the heart's embrace, the love we share.
For in each moment, we find our place,
In this mosaic of divine grace.

With open hearts, let us reveal,
The sacred journey, the wounds that heal.
For through this tapestry, we find our kin,
In the radiant mosaic of the divine within.

Reflections of Covenant

In the quiet hour of prayer,
Hearts lifted up, burdens laid bare.
Promises written in sacred ink,
In silent communion, we pause and think.

Winds of faith whisper through trees,
Carrying prayers upon gentle breeze.
Covenants forged in love so pure,
From trials endured, we find the cure.

Each moment bathed in holy light,
Guiding the weary through the night.
In each heartbeat, a sacred bond,
From the shadows, we feel Him respond.

Beneath the stars, we stand as one,
In the warmth of grace, our journey begun.
Through struggles and strife, we shall see,
The reflection of faith that sets us free.

Together we rise, united in song,
To the rhythm of blessings, we all belong.
In the tapestry of life, intertwined,
In the covenant of love, forever aligned.

The Graceful Wound

In the depths of sorrow, a seed is sown,
From every heartache, a light is grown.
Wounds, though painful, can teach us grace,
In the arms of mercy, we find our place.

Each scar a testament to battles fought,
In surrender, we learn what we sought.
Beauty arises from ashes of pain,
In the darkness, we embrace His reign.

With every tear that falls from the eye,
Hope emerges, as time passes by.
The wound may linger, yet love remains,
In the dance of healing, joy finds its gains.

A tapestry woven with threads of despair,
Yields a masterpiece, formed with care.
In the fabric of life, a story unfolds,
Through graceful wounds, we find what's told.

So we carry our scars, proud and high,
As reminders of grace, we reach for the sky.
In the heart of the storm, we gain our sight,
Through the graceful wound, we step into light.

Unseen Pilgrimage

Beneath the surface, a journey abounds,
In the heartbeat of silence, His love resounds.
Though the path is unclear, faith guides our way,
In the unseen pilgrimage, we learn to sway.

Each step we take, anchored in prayer,
Voices of angels whisper, 'We care.'
Through valleys of doubt, we tread with trust,
In the shadows of night, we rise from dust.

The compass of soul leads, though unseen,
Through trials and triumphs, life's in-between.
In every stumble, we find His hand,
A guiding light, where we boldly stand.

With every heartbeat, the journey unfolds,
Mapping the sacred in stories retold.
Together we walk, never alone,
On this unseen pilgrimage, love is our own.

So let us embrace the mystery near,
With faith as our armor, we conquer fear.
In the tapestry woven of hope and grace,
We find our belonging in our sacred space.

Divine Intricacies

In the threads of creation, a pattern divine,
Lies the essence of love, intricately entwined.
Through every heartbeat and each gentle sigh,
God's masterpiece glimmers in the vast sky.

In the wilderness, whispers of truth call,
Through the grandeur of mountains, in the shadows, we crawl.
Every detail crafted with purpose and care,
In the dance of the cosmos, His presence is rare.

From the petals of flowers to the stars' distant glow,
Every miracle crafted, a wonder to bestow.
In the depths of our hearts, His handiwork lies,
Reflecting the wisdom that time never denies.

Each moment a brushstroke on life's sacred canvas,
In the gallery of nature, we find our solace.
Divine intricacies, a symphony grand,
Guiding us gently with a Masterful hand.

So let us discover the beauty we find,
In the depth of our spirit, in the ties that bind.
In the divine intricacies, our souls take flight,
Awakening the wonder and love in our sight.

Reflections of Blessing

In the dawn's gentle light, we rise,
With hearts open wide, seeking the skies.
In every breath, a whispered prayer,
In the stillness, Your love we share.

Through trials faced and burdens borne,
Your grace, a cloak, in silence worn.
With grateful hearts, we join in song,
In unity, we all belong.

The rivers flow with sacred grace,
Through every wound, we find Your face.
A blessing wrapped in humble hands,
In every moment, Your love stands.

From valleys deep to mountains high,
Your light, our truth, we can't deny.
In echoes of faith, we softly tread,
For in Your name, our spirits are fed.

We gather close, in sacred trust,
In love's embrace, we rise when crushed.
Together, we embrace the call,
In reflections of blessing, we stand tall.

Threads of Hope

In the tapestry of life, we weave,
Threads of hope that help us believe.
Each color bright, a story told,
Of faith and love, in hearts we hold.

Through darkest nights, the stars align,
A guiding light, Your love divine.
With every stitch, a prayer we make,
In unity, our spirits awake.

The fabric stretches, sometimes frayed,
Yet in our weakness, strength displayed.
With hands outstretched, we lift each other,
In threads of hope, we find our mother.

In every struggle, a lesson learned,
With kindness given, our hearts discerned.
For woven tight in life's embrace,
The threads of hope shall find their place.

We walk together, hand in hand,
On this journey, together we stand.
With every thread, our faith we claim,
In a world transformed, we share Your name.

Unraveled Yet Whole

In shadows cast by doubt and fear,
We find the strength to persevere.
Though life may fray our fragile threads,
In sacred trust, our spirit spreads.

When storms arise and tempests rage,
In every heart, we turn the page.
For in the chaos, a quiet voice,
Calls us forth to lift and rejoice.

Each wound we bear, a badge of grace,
In moments lost, we find our place.
Though unraveled, we learn to cope,
In love's embrace, we find our hope.

Together bound, though torn apart,
In every scar, a brand new start.
For in the journey, we are whole,
Reflections of light within the soul.

In every step, with heads held high,
We seek the truth, we learn to fly.
Unraveled yet, in love we stand,
In Your embrace, we understand.

Celestial Remnants

In twilight's glow, the stars appear,
Whispers of grace, we hold them near.
Each flicker a promise, cosmic and bright,
Guiding our hearts through the velvet night.

Through cosmic dance, we find our way,
Celestial remnants, in skies so gray.
Your love, a beacon, forever shines,
In the galaxy of our intertwined lines.

The moonlight casts a silver hue,
Illuminating paths that lead us true.
With every heartbeat, we hear the call,
In celestial remnants, we stand tall.

From stardust born, we rise once more,
In harmony, forever we soar.
For in the heavens, our souls reside,
In faith and love, we shall abide.

In every star that lights the night,
In the quiet moments, we find our might.
Celestial remnants, woven as one,
Together we shine, until the day is done.

Notes of a Broken Hallelujah

In shadows deep, my soul does sing,
A fractured note, a whispered wing.
Yet in the pain, a spark of light,
A broken song, still takes its flight.

Through hollow cries, the spirit yearns,
For every tear, a lesson learns.
In silent prayers, my heart finds peace,
Embracing flaws, my soul's release.

The echoes of despair resound,
Yet grace ignites the holy ground.
With every stumble, faith's embrace,
A hallelujah, in the grace.

In darkness, hope, a flickering flame,
In weary hearts, we seek His name.
The melody of life's refrain,
A broken song, yet whole again.

And as the dawn begins to break,
A symphony, my heart must make.
For in this life, with all its strife,
The notes of love breathe breath to life.

In the Garden of My Heart

Among the blooms, my spirit grows,
In tender soil, where mercy flows.
With every seed, a promise sown,
In faith's embrace, I am not alone.

Through withered leaves and thorns of pain,
I find the strength in every rain.
In quiet whispers of the night,
The starry sky, a guiding light.

Each petal soft, a prayer ascends,
In gratitude, my heart transcends.
With every fragrance sweetly spread,
I kneel in grace where angels tread.

The harvest comes, not in despair,
But in the love that fills the air.
Among the weeds, my soul takes flight,
In the garden, I find my light.

So tend this soil, both rich and bare,
For in this heart, I lay my care.
A sanctuary for the soul,
In God's embrace, I am made whole.

Reverent Ruins

In crumbling stone, the shadows dwell,
A story whispered, a silent bell.
Where faith once stood, now dust remains,
Yet echoes linger, in sacred chains.

Through weathered walls, the light breaks through,
A testament to what was true.
In every crack, a tale unfolds,
Of divine love that never folds.

What seems like loss, is grace in disguise,
In reverent ruins, the spirit flies.
Amid the ashes of yesterday,
Hope rises up, to light the way.

The remnants speak of trials faced,
A sacred ground, the heart embraced.
In fragile forms, we find our peace,
In broken hearts, our souls release.

So let the ruins tell their tales,
Of love's endurance, that never fails.
For in our scars, the light comes in,
A reverent place, where we begin.

The Holy Within the Hurt

In every wound, the spirit weeps,
Yet in that pain, a promise keeps.
Through tears that fall like gentle rain,
A holy love that soothes the pain.

Amidst the trials, strength is born,
In darkest hours, a light is worn.
With every breath, the heart will sing,
Of hope reborn, and love's offering.

The scars we bear, a sacred mark,
In softened whispers, where dreams spark.
Each heavy heart, a chance to rise,
To see the holy in our sighs.

So let the hurt be not in vain,
For in the struggle, love remains.
With open arms, we face the storm,
And in the hurt, we are reborn.

For every shadow hides a light,
A gift of grace in darkest night.
The holy dwells where pain is found,
In every heartbeat, love unbound.

Sacred Shatters

In the quiet of the morn, we seek,
Echoes of the divine, softly speak.
Each shard of light, a sacred kiss,
Whispers of grace, a moment of bliss.

Fragile hearts, in awe, unwind,
Finding peace, where love is blind.
In shattered pieces, whole we find,
The thread of faith, endlessly intertwined.

A chorus of hope, resoundingly clear,
In a world of chaos, we draw near.
From brokenness, new life may grow,
In the light of truth, we fervently sow.

Through trials and tears, our spirits soar,
In the depths of despair, we explore.
Each sacred shatter, a step to grace,
In the arms of love, we find our place.

With reverence, we gather, hand in hand,
In the temple of hearts, together we stand.
Through sacred shatters, our souls align,
In the dance of creation, forever divine.

Remnants of Reverence

In the hush of twilight, shadows blend,
Soft memories linger, as night descends.
Each reverent breath, a prayer to the stars,
Carrying whispers of our hidden scars.

Fragments of faith, scattered with grace,
In the tapestry of time, we find our place.
Through trials faced, we rise anew,
In the warmth of love, we'll see it through.

Graffiti of life on the walls of the soul,
Speaking of journeys that make us whole.
From remnants of reverence, a story unfolds,
In sacred silence, our truth is told.

Lit by the fire of hope's gentle blaze,
We honor the past while embracing the praise.
In each gentle heart, a canvas so wide,
Remnants of reverence, forever our guide.

Let us gather the fragments, treasure them dear,
For in each remembrance, a purpose is clear.
With compassion and love, we'll walk the road,
In the strength of our spirits, together we've strode.

The Soul's Tapestry

In colors of dawn, the threads intertwine,
Weaving together the sacred design.
Every heartbeat, a note in the song,
In the dance of existence, where we belong.

Patterned with joy, and stitched with our pain,
The soul's true essence, in sunshine and rain.
Each moment a thread, in luminous hue,
Crafting a story of me and of you.

In the weft of the world, a vision unfolds,
A tapestry rich with tales long told.
With love as the needle, our spirits align,
In the fabric of being, our hearts intertwine.

Through shadows and light, the textures unfold,
A sacred creation, both humble and bold.
In the strands of our lives, we find our way home,
In the soul's tapestry, we're never alone.

So cherish each thread, for they weave our fate,
In the grand design, we celebrate.
With gratitude guiding our every embrace,
In the artistry of life, we find our grace.

Illuminated Shadows

In the twilight, where shadows play,
Light dances softly, chasing dread away.
In illuminated shadows, truth takes flight,
A journey through darkness, toward the light.

Each sigh of the night, a prayer we send,
In the arms of the silence, where spirits mend.
With every shadow, a story born,
In the interplay of dusk, we are reborn.

The gentle embrace of the moon's soft glow,
Meanders through paths where our secrets flow.
In illuminated shadows, fears dissolve,
Quenching our thirst, in love's resolve.

As the stars twinkle bright, our hearts ignite,
In the fabric of dreams, we hold on tight.
Illuminated shadows, guiding our way,
In the night's tender arms, we choose to stay.

Through the veils of the past, we rise and we bend,
With each illuminated shadow, we comprehend.
In the weave of our journeys, we find our song,
In luminous darkness, we all belong.

Harmony in the Chaos

In shadows deep, where whispers dwell,
A sacred light begins to swell.
The heart finds peace amidst the storm,
In chaos, grace begins to warm.

When burdens heavy weigh the soul,
Trust in the voice that makes us whole.
Each trial sings a holy song,
In every note, we all belong.

The winds shall shift, the path unclear,
Yet faith will guide us, calm our fear.
In every tear, a seed is sown,
In darkened nights, we find our own.

Harmony blooms in disarray,
As night surrenders into day.
With open hearts and spirits bold,
The truth of love shall be retold.

Together we stand, hand in hand,
In unity, we greet the land.
Divine connections, woven tight,
Create a tapestry of light.

Anointed Echoes

In whispered prayers, the spirits rise,
Anointed echoes fill the skies.
With each heartbeat, we seek the flame,
To honor the sacred, share the name.

In silence found, the truth unfolds,
A story written in the folds.
Through trials faced and shadows cast,
The light of hope forever lasts.

Voices lifted, praise declared,
In every struggle, love is shared.
The anointed find their rightful place,
In every corner, seek His grace.

In the rhythm of the night,
We gather strength and share the light.
With open arms, we welcome all,
To rise together, never fall.

Each soul a note in heaven's song,
In unity, we all belong.
Anointed echoes ring so clear,
A symphony for all to hear.

The Cherished Condemnation

In shadows thrown by judgment's hand,
We find a love that helps us stand.
The heart, though bruised, shall learn to mend,
In every fault, we find a friend.

Condemnation holds but fleeting power,
While grace and mercy bloom like flowers.
In scars we wear, the stories shine,
A cherished path, by design divine.

In every tear, a lesson learned,
The fires stoked, our spirits burned.
Yet from the ashes, hope will soar,
In brokenness, we find much more.

Each moment spent in pain's embrace,
Transforms the heart, reveals His face.
With open hands, we share the weight,
In love, we rewrite every fate.

Together, we shall rise above,
Cherished in the depths of love.
Condemnation fades, replaced by grace,
In every heart, we find our place.

Wholeness in the Fracture

In every crack, a glimmer shines,
The brokenness, a gift divine.
Embrace the flaws, the edges rough,
Within the pain, we find what's tough.

Wholeness grows where fractures lie,
In tender hearts, we'll learn to fly.
Each jagged piece tells of the fight,
A tapestry woven, pure and bright.

In night's embrace, we seek the dawn,
Through trials faced, we carry on.
The grace appears, in darkest hours,
Transforming pain to sacred powers.

We gather strength from every scar,
In love's embrace, we travel far.
Together walking, hand in hand,
In unity, we take our stand.

Wholeness found in every trial,
In fractured moments, we reconcile.
With open hearts, we rise anew,
In every challenge, love breaks through.

Celestial Invitations

Stars whisper softly in the night,
Guiding the weary to the light.
Angels beckon with their grace,
Inviting hearts to a sacred place.

Clouds part gently, a path revealed,
In the silence, truth is healed.
Heaven's door opens wide,
Welcoming all who seek to abide.

Beneath the moon's eternal glow,
Hope flourishes, faith will grow.
Each breath a prayer, each step a call,
In celestial love, we rise, not fall.

Echoes of joy, a melody pure,
In devotion's bond, we find our cure.
Hands lifted high, we sing a hymn,
In the light of love, our fears grow dim.

With hearts aligned, we find our way,
Transcending night, embracing day.
Celestial songs, our spirits soar,
Through every trial, forevermore.

Pilgrim's Heart

A pilgrim wanders, seeking truth,
With every step, rekindles youth.
Paths of dust beneath their feet,
Footprints whisper where they meet.

Morning dew on grass so bright,
Guides the heart in search of light.
In the silence, they find grace,
In every challenge, a warm embrace.

Mountains high and valleys deep,
In faith's embrace, the soul will leap.
Light the candles, burn them low,
In every flicker, love will grow.

Hands outstretched to the sky,
Offering prayers as they pass by.
In the night, they find their spark,
A guiding star against the dark.

Gathered in circle, voices raised,
In unity, the heart is praised.
Each breath a bond, a sacred art,
In the journey, the pilgrim's heart.

Altar of Remnants

Upon the altar, memories rest,
Fragments of time that we invest.
Each tear a treasure, each sigh a song,
In the silence, we belong.

Candlelight flickers, shadows dance,
In every challenge, find your stance.
Offering whispers of love and pain,
In the valley, beauty will reign.

Echoes of laughter, shadows of tears,
Gathered together through all our years.
In the fragments, we see the whole,
In every story, there lies a goal.

Time holds secrets, a gentle guide,
In moments shared, we stand with pride.
Breathe in the light, breathe out the night,
In the remnants, we find our sight.

Each relic a lesson, each stone a prayer,
In the unity of love, we find our care.
Altar of remnants, our hearts entwined,
In every heartbeat, divinely aligned.

Divine Echoes

In the stillness, echoes ring,
Whispers of love that heavens bring.
Moments linger, soft and clear,
In every breath, we feel You near.

Waves of light, a gentle touch,
In every heartbeat, love is such.
Divine presence flows like a stream,
In silent prayer, we dare to dream.

Crossing paths with sacred souls,
In the unity, the spirit unfolds.
Together we stand, hand in hand,
In every echo, a promised land.

Through the tempest, through the storm,
Divine whispers keep us warm.
Guiding us back to love's embrace,
In the echoes, we find our place.

Songs of praise rise to the skies,
In every note, the spirit flies.
Divine echoes, forever strong,
In the heart's melody, we belong.

Sunday Reflections

In quiet moments, we gather near,
With hearts open wide, we cast off fear.
Whispers of grace through the sunlight gleam,
In the stillness, we find our dream.

The hymn of hope dances through the air,
Lifted by love, we rise from despair.
Each prayer echoes in the sacred space,
A testament of faith intertwined with grace.

Together we walk on this holy ground,
In the warmth of fellowship, solace is found.
Voices in harmony, spirits entwined,
In Sunday reflections, pure truth we find.

With gratitude deep, we elevate our souls,
In unity's embrace, we are made whole.
Each moment a gift, each life a song,
In the light of the Lord, we always belong.

As the sun sets low, with hearts aglow,
We cherish the love that begins to flow.
In memories cherished, we seek to see,
The beauty of Sunday, where souls roam free.

Sacred Journeys

Step by step, we walk the path,
Guided by whispers, avoiding the wrath.
Each footprint a prayer, each breath a song,
In the depths of our hearts, we learn to be strong.

Mountains may rise, and valleys may fall,
But faith as our compass, we answer the call.
With hands intertwined, we traverse the way,
In sacred journeys, where hope lights the day.

The stars are our beacons, the moon our guide,
In the vastness of night, with love we abide.
Each challenge a lesson, each storm a grace,
Through sacred journeys, we find our place.

Voices of wisdom echo through time,
In the tapestry of life, we find our rhyme.
With hearts ever open, and spirits so bright,
In the warmth of the sacred, we bask in the light.

Through rivers of trials, we dance and we swim,
For faith is the bridge, when the light grows dim.
Together in spirit, we journey through years,
In sacred journeys, we conquer our fears.

Enigmatic Prayers

In shadows profound where silence resides,
I seek for the answers that the heart hides.
An enigmatic prayer whispers my name,
As the soul reaches out through the flickering flame.

Heavenly echoes surround me tonight,
In the stillness, I sense a divine light.
Mysteries woven in soft, gentle sighs,
Each prayer a quest for the truth that fulfills.

With eyes full of wonder and hearts full of grace,
I ponder the journey, the eternal chase.
In moments of doubt, I raise my plea high,
To the realms where our spirits can freely fly.

Lost in the tapestry, threads intertwined,
Are answers to questions, so patiently refined.
Enigmatic prayers rise like stars in the night,
Each call from the heart, a spark of the light.

As dawn breaks anew, bathed in soft grace,
The enigmatic silence transforms the space.
With hope as my anchor, I rise on the day,
In the dance of existence, forever I'll stay.

Threads of Eternity

In the fabric of time, we weave our dreams,
Threads of eternity unravel at seams.
Each moment a stitch in the grand design,
Guided by love, through the sacred divine.

With every breath drawn, we anchor our souls,
In the tapestry of life, where the spirit unfolds.
Colors of laughter, and shades of our tears,
Within the threads woven, we conquer our fears.

As seasons may change and the years swiftly flow,
In the warmth of connection, love starts to grow.
Threads of eternity, faithfully spun,
In the journey of hope, we become ever one.

Through trials and triumphs, in shadow and light,
The fibers of faith guide us through the night.
With hearts intertwined, and visions so clear,
Threads of eternity unite us, sincere.

In every heartbeat, the whispers of grace,
In the grand design, we each find our place.
Together in spirit, our voices will soar,
In the threads of eternity, forever explore.

Heart's Confession

In silence I kneel, my spirit bare,
Before the altar of love and care.
With every tear that falls like rain,
I seek Your grace to heal my pain.

Whispers of mercy fill the air,
Forgiveness blooms in answered prayer.
In shadows deep, Your light appears,
Calming the tempest of my fears.

Lord, I lay my burdens down,
In Your embrace, I lose my frown.
With humbled heart, I seek to find,
The peace You offer, pure and kind.

Each flaw, each wound, I bring to You,
In faith, I trust You'll make me new.
In every doubt, in every sigh,
Help me to rise, and learn to fly.

So in this heart's confession, dear,
I feel Your presence drawing near.
With open arms, I'm not alone,
In every breath, I've made You known.

Crown of Thorns

Upon His brow, the sharp thorns pressed,
A symbol of love, in pain, confessed.
He bore the weight of sin and scorn,
From darkest night to brightest morn.

Each drop of blood, a price so dear,
In suffering, He held us near.
With every lash that struck His skin,
He breathed forgiveness for our sin.

The crown He wore, a gift of grace,
Transforming wrath into embrace.
In agony, He chose to save,
A path of love, the world would pave.

Through trials faced, we find our way,
In shadows deep, He is our stay.
With hope imbued in every heart,
His love remains, we'll never part.

So let us wear our crowns of pain,
With faith that blossoms in the rain.
In every thorn, a story told,
Of love divine, more precious than gold.

Blooming Roses

In gardens lush, where roses sway,
Their colors bright, a soft ballet.
Each petal whispers prayers of praise,
Inviting souls to lift their gaze.

The fragrance sweet, a heavenly sign,
In every bloom, Your love divine.
Through trials faced, we find our grace,
In nature's arms, we seek Your face.

With roots that dig deep in the earth,
They flourish bright, renewed in worth.
In every thorn, the lesson lies,
That beauty stems from sacrifice.

So let us tend the garden bright,
With hands that nurture, hearts that light.
For in each rose, a promise grows,
Of love eternal, where hope flows.

In every season, let us see,
The blooming roses set us free.
A testament of faith and love,
Reflecting grace from skies above.

The Anatomy of Hope

Hope is a seed we plant with care,
In the soil of faith, it grows aware.
With roots that stretch through trials faced,
In every heart, Your love embraced.

The sun that shines on dreams at night,
Guides weary souls towards the light.
In every doubt, a chance to stand,
With open arms, we make our plans.

Hope is a song, soft, sweet, and clear,
Resonating words that calm our fear.
In darkest hours, it lifts our eyes,
To greater truths, where mercy lies.

In moments lost, when paths divide,
Hope is the compass, love the guide.
With every beat, our spirits rise,
Anchored in faith, beyond the skies.

So let us weave this tapestry,
Of hope and love in harmony.
In every breath, with joy we cope,
For life is bright, and filled with hope.

Prayers in Disguise

In whispered hopes, our hearts confide,
With every tear, we pray inside.
In silence spoken, love revealed,
The brokenness, a heart now healed.

When words escape, and doubts arise,
Our spirits lift in prayerful sighs.
For in the silence, faith takes flight,
Transforming shadows into light.

Each burden shared, a testament,
Of love unspoken, heaven-sent.
In moments frail, we find our voice,
In prayers disguised, our hearts rejoice.

Let every pain become a plea,
A bridge that spans eternity.
In every struggle, strength cascades,
Like rivers flowing, hope parades.

So as we walk this sacred path,
In prayers of love, we find our faith.
For every sigh and tear that falls,
Are prayers in disguise, love's gentle calls.

The Journey Within

In silence deep, the spirit seeks,
A whisper soft in shadowed peaks.
The heart unfolds, a sacred space,
To find the light, the soul's embrace.

With every breath, a step is made,
Through valleys lost, in twilight's shade.
Each moment, like a prayerful sigh,
A dance with truth that will not die.

The path grows clear, the vision bright,
Through trials faced, emerges light.
With each return, the lessons learned,
The flame of faith within us burned.

In stillness found, the journey's grace,
Reflects the love in every face.
Together bound, we walk as one,
In quest of peace when day is done.

So trust the way, the heart's intent,
In every step, a life well spent.
For in the depths, the truth will sing,
The journey's heart will ever bring.

Essence of Benediction

O gentle breeze, through branches sway,
A heartfelt prayer, as night greets day.
In sacred words, our hopes ascend,
A song of love that will not end.

The sun that shines on fields below,
Gifts us the strength to learn and grow.
With every dawn, a chance anew,
To breathe in grace, to seek the true.

In every smile, a blessing shared,
The bonds of faith, forever pared.
In kindness shown, our hearts align,
A tapestry of love, divine.

Through trials faced and burdens borne,
A still small voice, in us reborn.
With every tear, a drop of peace,
In love's embrace, our sorrows cease.

So lift your hands, let praises rise,
In every heart, the Spirit lies.
Together we, in grace, will stand,
Essence of love, hand in hand.

Pilgrim's Echoes

We wander forth on paths unknown,
With hearts of stone turned into bone.
In echoes of the past we hear,
The whispers soft, the call is clear.

Through winding roads and sunlit glades,
The pilgrim's heart in truth parades.
With every step, the world unfolds,
A tale of faith and love retold.

Each challenge faced, the spirit grows,
In trials met, resilience shows.
The echoes hum in twilight's glow,
In seeking peace, our spirits flow.

Beneath the stars, we find our way,
In silence deep, we pause and pray.
The sacred fire within us burns,
For every soul, the lesson learns.

So side by side, we journey on,
Under the watchful gaze of dawn.
In every heart, a pilgrim's song,
An echo sweet, where we belong.

Divine Reflections

In tranquil streams, the heavens gleam,
A mirror bright, a sacred dream.
Each ripple shows the world anew,
In whispers soft, the spirit's view.

From mountains high to valleys low,
The divine light begins to flow.
In nature's grace, we find the thread,
Of love that lives where angels tread.

The clouds above, like dreams they drift,
An artist's hand, a holy gift.
In every color, truth reveals,
A touch of grace that softly heals.

Through storms we face, in shadows cast,
The strength of faith will ever last.
In trials met and hopes regained,
Divine reflections, love unchained.

So gather close, in light we'll dwell,
With open hearts, all will be well.
In every soul, a spark divine,
Reflections of the love, we shine.

Divine Reflections

In still waters, echoes flow,
Whispers of grace, soft and low.
Hearts aligned in sacred space,
Finding light in every trace.

Faith blooms brightly, pure and true,
Guided by love in all we do.
Hands entwined, we walk the way,
Uniting souls in bright array.

Each moment shines, a holy gift,
In trials met, our spirits lift.
Through shadows deep, we seek the day,
With trust unwavering, we'll not stray.

The path unfolds, a sacred quest,
In every heart, a promise dressed.
Together rise, as one we sing,
In harmony, His praises ring.

Embracing hope, a burning flame,
In whispered prayers, we speak His name.
With every tear, a lesson found,
In Divine love, forever bound.

Fractured Light

In shattered glass, His image gleams,
Broken pieces, yet shining dreams.
From the cracks, His spirit spills,
Healing hearts, and bending wills.

Through night's embrace, a candle glows,
A flicker of faith, where love still flows.
In darkness deep, we find our way,
With fractured light, we choose to stay.

Each scar and wound, a story told,
Of grace anew, from ashes bold.
In tangled paths, His truth we find,
Fractured hearts, forever aligned.

The dawn shall break, its colors wide,
In vibrant hues, where hope abides.
We rise as one, with voices raised,
In fractured light, He is praised.

With joy anew, we dance in peace,
In brokenness, we find release.
Together we stand, our spirits bright,
In the warmth of His guiding light.

Chosen in the Fragments

In every shard, a truth revealed,
A sacred story, gently healed.
We gather pieces, hearts conjoined,
In every fragment, love enshrined.

Through trials faced, and storms we tread,
In shattered dreams, His voice is bred.
Embracing loss, we find our song,
In chosen fragments, we belong.

With weary hands, we shape our fate,
In every struggle, His hands create.
Forged through fire, our spirits rise,
In brokenness, our faith supplies.

The puzzle's set, His wisdom clear,
In every corner, grace draws near.
We find in fragments, vibrant whole,
A masterpiece, our shared soul.

Together we weave a tapestry bright,
In unity's bond, we find our light.
For in the pieces, love ignites,
Chosen in the fragments, His light invites.

Mosaic of the Spirit

Each soul a tile, unique and bright,
Together forming endless light.
In loving hues, we intertwine,
Creating beauty, divine design.

Through each potential, we embrace,
The radiant truth of His grace.
With open hearts, we choose to see,
The mosaic born from you and me.

In gentle whispers, wisdom sings,
In every note, the Spirit clings.
Through laughter shared and tears that flow,
The mosaic shines, our love we show.

Each fragment holds a sacred part,
A testament of every heart.
In unity, our spirits soar,
Creating peace forevermore.

In vibrant colors, we unite,
Our diverse paths converge in light.
In the harmony of His embrace,
We find our place, our sacred space.

Secrets of The Sacred

In quiet places, spirits sigh,
Where faith ignites the holy sky.
Beneath the stars, the whispers dwell,
In sacred vows, we hear them tell.

The truths of old, they guide the heart,
In shadows cast, they play their part.
With prayers woven through sacred trees,
The light of hope flows with the breeze.

In every tear, a lesson learned,
Through burning fires, our souls are turned.
Unseen hands, they lead us home,
In silent moments, we are not alone.

The echoes of the faithful past,
In whispered dreams, we're held steadfast.
Through trials deep, we rise in grace,
In every struggle, faith finds its place.

Embrace the light, let shadows flee,
In unity, we come to see.
The sacred secrets softly hum,
In every heart, God's kingdom comes.

Faith in the Fissures

In cracks of doubt, the light breaks through,
A fragile hope, so pure and true.
In every heart, a struggle lies,
Yet faith emerges, it never dies.

Through trials faced, the soul will grow,
In darkest nights, new strength will show.
Amidst the chaos, peace will reign,
In faith's embrace, we bear the pain.

From fissures deep, the spirit sings,
In brokenness, we find new wings.
Through storms we weather, hand in hand,
In every stride, God's truth will stand.

Let courage bloom where fear resides,
In every heart, the light abides.
For every fracture leads the way,
To paths of hope that guide our stay.

In every crack, a vision bright,
Trust in the dawn, the coming light.
Through shadows cast, our spirits soar,
In faith we rise, forevermore.

Whispers from the Wounded

Beneath the scars, a story breathes,
In every pain, a wisdom weaves.
The wounded heart, it softly speaks,
In gentle tones, the spirit seeks.

Through shattered dreams, we learn to see,
The grace that flows, the unity.
In every tear, a lesson found,
In whispers low, our hopes rebound.

In silence held, the truth unfolds,
Through battles fought, the heart grows bold.
The pain of loss, a sacred gift,
In every crack, the spirits lift.

Let healing hands bring forth the light,
In darkest valleys, love ignites.
The whispers rise, they break the night,
In wounded hearts, we find our might.

For every wound, a chance to grow,
In every struggle, seeds we sow.
In fractured souls, a bond is made,
In whispers soft, our fears shall fade.

Reverberations of the Redeemed

In echoes sweet, redemption calls,
Through shadows deep, the spirit thralls.
From ashes rise, the faithful stand,
In reverence, we seek His hand.

The chains that bind, they fall away,
As love restores, we see the day.
Through trials faced, the heart finds peace,
In every burden, burdens cease.

With voices raised, we lift our song,
Of grace bestowed, where we belong.
In unity, the choir grows,
In every heart, the spirit flows.

Let every life be marked by light,
In darkest moments, faith takes flight.
Through every trial, we find our way,
In blessed hope, we choose to stay.

In whispers soft, the past released,
In love embraced, our souls are blessed.
Reverberations of the saved,
In every heart, His love engraved.

The Crossroads of Identity

At the crossroads, souls converge,
Turning dreams to sacred paths,
In whispers, truths emerge,
Finding solace in His grace.

A journey of heart and mind,
In faith, we seek to know,
The purpose we long to find,
As holy winds begin to blow.

In shadows, we paint our fears,
But light brings clarity's gift,
Through trials, our vision clears,
As spirits rise and hearts uplift.

With every step, redemption calls,
Fear fades beneath His gaze,
In unity, our spirit thralls,
As hope ignites, we sing His praise.

At the crossroads, we are whole,
Bound together, hand in hand,
In the light of love, we stroll,
Finding peace in His command.

Nectar of the Spirit

In the garden of the soul,
Where blossoms grace the boughs,
The nectar flows, making us whole,
A divine love that always allows.

With every drop, the heart expands,
Sipped from vessels pure and bright,
Uniting life through gentle hands,
Guiding lost souls to the light.

Sweet melodies of prayer arise,
In harmony with heaven's choir,
Through patience, truth defies,
And ignites within our fire.

We gather 'neath the starlit skies,
As gratitude consumes the night,
With open hearts, we realize,
The nectar brings eternal light.

Each drop a sign, a sacred bond,
An invitation to be free,
In spirit's dance, we joyously respond,
To the love that flows eternally.

Fragments of Love

In shards of light, love glimmers bright,
Each fragment tells a sacred tale,
A tapestry woven through day and night,
Where grace and sorrow intertwine and sail.

Moments captured, never lost,
In every smile, a memory stays,
A reminder of love's gentle cost,
Through trials faced, it always sways.

In whispers soft, a kind embrace,
The heart finds comfort, a love divine,
Each fragment holds a holy place,
Eternity gleams where paths align.

Through tears and joy, we celebrate,
The beauty that emerges from pain,
In unity, we elevate,
Fragments of love shall always reign.

In the silence, love's echo thunders,
Resonating deep within the soul,
Amidst the trials, it never blunders,
For in love's fragments, we feel whole.

Echoes of the Past

In quiet moments, echoes rise,
Voices of those who came before,
In whispers soft, the spirit sighs,
Guiding paths to an open door.

With every heartbeat, tales unfold,
Of strength, of hope, of lessons learned,
Wisdom flows from days of old,
As souls unite, the heart is turned.

Through trials faced, the spirits guide,
In shadows cast, their light remains,
In every step, we take in stride,
Their courage flows through joys and pains.

The past, a tapestry so rich,
We stand on shoulders broad and tall,
In gratitude, we find the stitch,
That binds us all, answering the call.

In echoes' grace, we rise and stand,
Embracing stories yet untold,
In unity, we clasp our hands,
For love endures, and never grows old.

Milton Keynes UK
Ingram Content Group UK Ltd.
UKHW021858151124
451262UK00014B/1325